Katy Perry

BY JAN BERNARD

The Child's World

Published by The Child's World®
1980 Lookout Drive • Mankato, MN 56003-1705
800-599-READ • www.childsworld.com

Acknowledgments
The Child's World®: Mary Berendes, Publishing Director
The Design Lab: Cover and interior design
Amnet: Cover and interior production
Red Line Editorial: Editorial direction

Photo credits
Helga Esteb/Shutterstock Images, cover, 1; Harmony
Gerber/Shutterstock Images, 5, 29; Jeff Kravitz/FilmMagic/
Getty Images, 7; Seth Poppel/Yearbook Library, 9; Dave
Newman/Shutterstock Images, 11; Victor Spinelli/WireImage/
Getty Images, 13; Daniel Portnoy/AP Images, 14; Amanda
Edwards/Getty Images, 16; Daniel Monterroso/Shutterstock
Images, 18; Matt Sayles/AP Images, 20; Joe Seer/Shutterstock
Images, 22; Ronald Zak/AP Images, 25; Debby Wong/
Shutterstock Images, 27

Design elements
Sergey Shvedov/iStockphoto

ISBN 9781614732938
LCCN 2012933734

Printed in the United States of America
Mankato, MN
July 2012
PA02128

Table of Contents

CHAPTER 1

A Little Bit Crazy

If you happen to see a woman with blue hair wearing candy-colored clothes and high heels, you might just be looking at Katy Perry. Katy is most famous for her singing. But she is also known for her creativity and silliness.

Katy calls herself an oddball. But she is indeed a pop music superstar. In fact, she became the first artist ever to have songs in the Billboard top ten for a full year. Famous television interviewer Barbara Walters called Katy one of the most fascinating people of 2011. So just who is Katy Perry?

Katy Perry performs in Los Angeles, California, in 2011.

CHAPTER 2

Gospel Music

Katheryn Elizabeth Hudson was born on October 25, 1984, in Santa Barbara, California. She has an older sister and younger brother. Her parents are Keith and Mary. They are both **evangelical** pastors. Her parents were very loving. However, they were also very **strict**.

Today Katy is a well-known pop star. As a kid, though, she was not even allowed to listen to pop music. Katy's parents only let her listen to **gospel music**. The first time Katy heard something else was at a slumber party. It was there that she heard the rock band Queen.

Katy fell in love with the sound and the beat. But gospel music continued to be her main focus for years to come. Katy's father would give her ten dollars to

Katy poses with her parents in 2010.

perform in her church and at local restaurants. Katy also took dance and singing lessons. She even studied **opera** for a little while. At 13, she took up the guitar. Katy spent hours at home practicing. She started writing her own songs, too.

Katy knew she wanted to become a singer and songwriter. So she left her high school after her freshman year. Katy still earned a high school diploma, though. But this way she could start her singing career more quickly.

Few would probably guess that Katy is a natural blond. She usually dyes her hair black. However, she wears lots of multicolored wigs, too. Katy has even dyed her hair blue!

Katy in her freshman year of high school

CHAPTER 3

A Rocky Start

Nashville, Tennessee, is known for its music industry. Katy's parents knew people in Nashville who worked in gospel music. So Katy went there at age 15. Mary went as well. They hoped Katy could get her start.

And indeed she did. Katy recorded an album in Nashville. It featured Christian music. She used her real name, Katy Hudson, on the album.

The album never had much of a chance. The record company went out of business soon after the album was released. Only a few copies had been sold at that point. Katy and Mary went back to Santa Barbara after that. But Katy was still determined to make it in the music business.

Katy moved to Nashville, Tennessee, to make gospel music.

CHAPTER 4

All About the Name

After returning to California, Katy took the name Katy Perry. There is a famous actress named Kate Hudson. Katy worried that Katy Hudson sounded too similar. She decided to use the last name Perry because it was her mother's maiden name.

Katy moved to Los Angeles, California, at age 17. Money was really tight for years. Katy's car was taken away when she could not make payments. She wrote some checks that bounced. That means she did not have money to pay the checks, so they could not be cashed. Katy even sold some of her own clothes just to earn money for rent. But she would not give up. Katy just knew she could make it.

Katy was determined to be successful in
Los Angeles, California.

CHAPTER 5

Never Give Up

Katy was able to work with Glen Ballard. He was a famous music **producer**. Among the artists Ballard

Glen Ballard worked with Katy on her music.

had worked with were Michael Jackson and Alanis Morissette.

It looked like Katy would finally get her big break in 2003. That is when she signed with Island Def Jam. It is a very important recording company. Everything seemed to be going well. Katy had an album of her own ready to release. She also made an album with the group Matrix. It had chosen her to be one of its lead female singers.

Then everything changed. Both albums were delayed just before they were to be released. Then the final blow came. Island Def Jam dropped her. Katy saw her dreams disappearing. But she still did not give up.

Columbia Records signed Katy in 2004. She hoped that meant things were turning around. Her song "Simple" was even featured in the movie *The Sisterhood of the Traveling Pants*. But Columbia decided not to release her album. It then dropped her from the label. This time, Katy started to think her dream might not happen.

Katy smiles while at a party in 2004.

CHAPTER 6

The Real Deal

People at Capitol Records heard Katy's music. They knew that she had the talent to make it big. So Capital Records signed Katy in 2007. It soon released her first single and breakout song, "I Kissed a Girl." The song received a boost when it was featured on a popular television show called *Gossip Girl*. It soon shot into the top 100 list.

In 2011, Katy was chosen to be the voice of Smurfette in the movie *The Smurfs*. She also has been a spokesperson for the companies Proactiv and Adidas.

"I Kissed a Girl" was on the top 100 list for seven weeks. It topped the charts in

Katy performed on the Warped Tour in 2008.

20 countries. Journalists started asking Katy to appear on television shows. She made a tour of radio stations, **promoting** her music. She also joined the Warped Tour. It was famous for its alternative rock bands and extreme sports performances. Katy hoped it would help her reach a new audience.

CHAPTER 7

Triple Platinum

Katy's popularity exploded in 2008. That is when her album *One of the Boys* was released. It quickly went to number nine on the charts. Her songs "I Kissed a Girl" and "Hot N Cold" made it to triple platinum. That means they sold more than three million copies each! Katy's parents might have been strict, but they supported Katy by appearing in her music video for "Hot N Cold."

Katy was "slimed" at the 2010 Nickelodeon Kids' Choice Awards. That is when slime is dumped onto somebody as a joke. Katy won the Favorite Female Singer award at the show.

Katy released her second album with Capitol Records in 2010. It was called *Teenage Dream*.

The album reached number one. The first hit song was called "California Gurls." Katy sang with rapper Snoop Dogg in the song. It was the number one song on the Billboard charts for six weeks.

Another hit song was called "Firework." Katy

Katy performs with rapper Snoop Dogg in 2010.

dedicated it to people who are bullied or feel like they do not belong. The song celebrates the specialness of everyone. The 250 people in the "Firework" video were not actors. They were Katy Perry fans!

CHAPTER 8

The Awards Start Coming

It didn't take long for the awards to pile up. Some honored Katy. She was named the Best New Act at the 2008 MTV Europe Awards. Then the BRIT Awards named her Best International Female Solo Artist in 2009. Other organizations honored her music. In 2010, "Hot N Cold" was **nominated** for the Best

Katy took her 90-year-old grandmother to the 2011 Grammy Awards show. Her grandmother had a sparkly cane. Katy wore angel wings. Katy has a great relationship with her grandmother. They tease each other all the time.

Katy's *Teenage Dream* album was nominated for Favorite Pop/Rock Album at the 2010 American Music Awards.

Female Pop Vocal Performance Grammy Award. Katy has even been honored for her music videos. "Firework" was named Video of the Year at the 2011 MTV Video Music Awards.

CHAPTER 9

Using Fame for Good

Katy supports many **charities** and causes. She once joined other music stars to put on a special concert for US soldiers. Katy also supports an organization called Tickets-for-Charity. Fans can purchase tickets to Katy's shows through that organization. Thanks to Katy, more than $175,000

Katy married actor Russell Brand in 2010. Their wedding was part of a six-day ceremony in India. However, they divorced 14 months later.

has been given to more than 50 charities. Some of those charities were the Humane Society of the United States and Generosity Water. Generosity Water builds water wells all over the world. The group helps people who otherwise would not have clean water.

Katy also supports St. Jude Children's Research Hospital and Music for Relief. She is pretty good to her fans, too. In November 2011, she performed a free concert for her fans in Los Angeles. Doing good sometimes means surprising people. Katy once surprised her fans in Australia when she showed up at their school prom. She sang Beyoncé's popular song "Single Ladies."

Katy performs at a charity concert in 2009 in Austria.

CHAPTER 10

Oh So Sweet

Katy's California Dreams Tour was one of a kind. It was a little like a cross between a trip to a candy factory and Disneyland. Floating candy clouds, dancing gingerbread men, and giant brownies filled the stage. There was enough giant ice cream and candy to make you drool.

Katy loves cats. Her own cat's name is Kitty Purry. In 2011 she introduced a perfume called Purr. It comes in a bottle shaped like a cat.

The California Dreams Tour was just like Katy's music. It is fun, often a little wacky, and makes fans want to jump up and dance.

Katy likes to use fun props and scenery at her concerts.

CHAPTER 11

A Long Career

Katy has said that she is a walking cartoon of herself. After all, she is well known for her outrageous behavior and outfits. Katy is happy about that, though. It is who she is.

It took Katy a lot of courage to stay on the road to success. That long journey turned out to be a good thing. Katy said it helps remind her to always enjoy the moment and to show her fans how much she appreciates them.

When Katy was 18, she got a Jesus tattoo on her wrist. Katy does not share the same beliefs as her parents. However, she knows she can look at that tattoo as a reminder of where she came from.

Katy is happy that she is able to express
herself through her music and performances.

GLOSSARY

charities (CHAR-i-tees): Charities are organizations that provide money or assistance to those in need. Katy helps others by giving to charities.

evangelical (ee-van-JEL-i-kuhl): Evangelical is a form of Christianity. Katy's parents were evangelical pastors.

gospel music (GAHS-puhl MYOO-zik): Gospel music relates to Christianity. Katy sang gospel music as a child.

nominated (NAH-muh-nate-id): To be named a finalist for an award is to be nominated. Katy's song "Hot N Cold" was nominated for an award.

opera (AH-pur-uh): Opera is a style of music in which the words are sung in a certain way. Katy once studied opera.

producer (pruh-DOOS-ur): A producer finds the money to make an album and supervises its production. Katy works with a producer when recording music.

promoting (pruh-MOTE-ing): Promoting means to support or encourage something. Katy talks to radio station deejays while promoting her music.

strict (STRIKT): A strict person wants rules to be obeyed exactly all the time. Katy's parents were strict during her childhood.

FURTHER INFORMATION

BOOKS

Adams, Michelle. *Katy Perry (Blue Banner Biographies)*. Hockessin, DE: Mitchell Lane Publishers, 2011.

Johnson, Robin. *Katy Perry (Superstars!)*. New York: Crabtree Publishing, 2011.

Stone, Dave. *Russell Brand & Katy Perry: The Love Story*. London UK: John Blake, 2010.

WEB SITES

Visit our Web site for links about Katy Perry: **childsworld.com/links**

Note to Parents, Teachers, and Librarians: We routinely verify our Web links to make sure they are safe and active sites. So encourage your readers to check them out!

INDEX

ABOUT THE AUTHOR

Jan Bernard has been an elementary teacher in both Ohio and in Georgia, and has written curriculum for schools for over seven years. She also is the author of seven books. She lives in West Jefferson, Ohio, with her husband and their dog, Nigel. She has two sons.